ONLY THE NAMES REMAIN

▼▲▼▲▼▲▼▲

The Cherokees and the Trail of Tears

▼▲▼▲▼▲▼▲

by Alex W. Bealer

Illustrated by Kristina Rodanas

LITTLE, BROWN AND COMPANY

Boston   New York   Toronto   London

Second Edition

ISBN 0-316-08518-9 (hc)
ISBN 0-316-08519-7 (pb)

LIBRARY OF CONGRESS CATALOG CARD NUMBER 71-169008

HC: 10 9 8 7 6 5 4 3 2 1
PB: 10 9 8 7 6 5 4 3 2 1

Printed in the United States of America

To BRYAN OWLE,
good friend, patient teacher
and Smoky Mountain companion
from my boyhood

— A. W. B.

CONTENTS

ONLY THE
NAMES REMAIN

▼▲▼▲▼▲▼▲

A Cherokee carved stone pipe

Cherokee Names

▼▲▼▲▼▲▼▲

The Chattahoochee River cuts across Georgia like the mark of a bright silver pencil. It serves as a boundary between the tall mountains to the north and the rolling foothills to the south.

Close to its banks one can see the southernmost mountain of the Appalachian range, Kennesaw Mountain. Beyond Kennesaw lies Oglethorpe Mountain and beyond that are shadowy ranges of countless more mountains which disappear in the distance.

There at Oglethorpe the ancient Appalachian

Trail begins. From Georgia this trail follows the highest ridges of the mountains northward until it disappears in the spruce and maple forests of Maine, a thousand miles or more away.

The mountain country of Georgia is a beautiful land now, as it has always been. It is also a peaceful land where campers pitch tents for the weekend, and fishermen cast for speckled trout in the rocky creeks. Prosperous farms are found in the valleys. But once, only a hundred and fifty years ago, this country was the scene of savage fighting. Soldiers armed with muskets marched along the mountain trails. Indians with rifles and bows and arrows shot at the soldiers from thickets of mountain laurel and rhododendron. Men were killed and children cried from fear and hunger. At that time the Chattahoochee was a boundary between two nations at war.

To the north, among the ageless wooded mountains, lived the Cherokee Nation, an independent nation with its own government and language and alphabet. The Cherokee Indians had lived in this land for almost a thousand years before Columbus discovered America. They had become a part of this country as much as wayah, the wolf; yonah, the bear; and tallalla, the woodpecker.

But south of the Chattahoochee lived the white man whose families had come to this new world from England and Scotland, Germany and France. They lived on land that had been conquered from the powerful Creek Nation, the Indians who had lived from the Chattahoochee south to Florida. These white men were numerous and powerful. They commanded armies of soldiers and operated blacksmith shops which made rifles and axes and shining steel knives. The white men wanted the Cherokees moved far to the west so that they and their sons could farm the fertile valleys of the Cherokee Nation.

The white man won. The Cherokees left the beautiful mountainous land of their ancestors. They were forced to live far away, in the West, which many of them felt was the home of evil spirits. Perhaps evil spirits did dwell in the new land, for the Cherokees were never the same again after they had left their mountains.

Now, no man alive in Georgia remembers the Cherokee Nation. The growing capital city of the Nation has been destroyed. There are no Cherokee women and girls left to pick the berries which grow along the creeks of the Georgia mountains. The deer which graze on the mountainsides are no more hunted by Cherokee men and boys. All that is left are names.

Some of the towns and rivers in North Georgia have names which sound like music and make one think of the time when Cherokees ruled this land. There is a small town named Hiawassee and another named Ellijay. Such names sound like the wind whispering in the mountain pines. Other towns are called Rising Fawn and Talking Rock and Ball Ground.

There are the rivers with strange names such as Chattahoochee, Oostenaula, Coosa, Chattooga and Etowah. Nacoochee is the name of a beautiful valley and Chattanooga the name of a great city.

These are Cherokee names, given to these places a thousand years before the white man came to America.

Now the Cherokees have gone. Only the names remain.

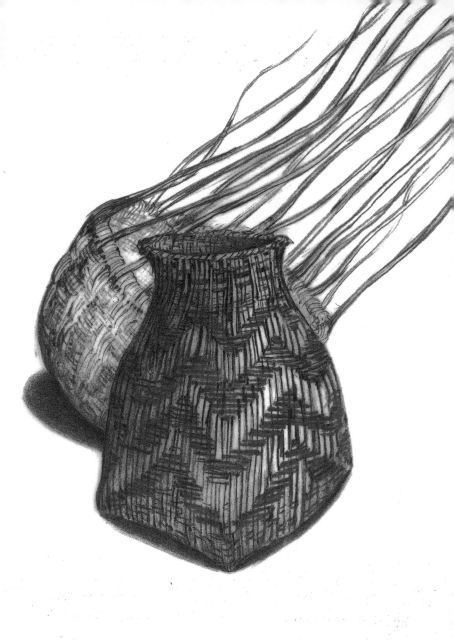

Cherokee-style baskets

Before the White Man

▼▲▼▲▼▲▼▲

Nobody knows exactly when the Cherokees came to the mountains of the South or where they came from. Since they speak a language much like that of the Iroquois Indians of New York, it is thought that they came from the North, long before the memory of the oldest man. When they reached what is now Georgia they stopped, for they were mountain people and liked the mountain country of the South.

The Cherokee men were fierce warriors. When they reached Georgia they fought the people who lived there. They burned the riverside villages of

the Mound Builders and used their rich fields for
their own gardens.

Cherokee legends also tell of the moon-eyed
men who moved into their country in those long-
ago times. These people had light skin and hair,
and blue eyes. It is possible that these moon-eyed
men were the descendants of the legendary
Welshman named Madoc, who sailed from the
British Isles about A.D. 1170 and disappeared in
the western sea. The Cherokees drove them into
the West and they were heard of no more. How
strange that the Cherokees themselves would be
driven westward in centuries to come, by men
with light skin and blue eyes.

Cherokee legends tell of how their land was
created. They say that once the earth was covered
with water which dried up and became mud. The
Great Buzzard, the father of all the buzzards
which now live, flew low over the mud to find a
dry place to live. When he grew tired he flew too
low and his wings hit the soft mud. Valleys were
created wherever his wings hit, and when he
raised his wings he created mountains. Cherokee

country has been mountainous since that time, the legends say.

Food was plentiful in the rich woodlands of the southern mountains. Buffalo and elk fed in the rich valleys, while deer and bear were numerous in the creek bottoms and on the mountainsides. Small game, such as rabbit, squirrel, groundhog and raccoon, was often hunted for food and fur. Huckleberries, blackberries and strawberries, sweet and delicious, grew thickly in clear spots along woodland trails and along the banks of rushing creeks. There were persimmons, crab apples, cherries and grapes to be gathered in season. Chestnuts, hickory nuts, black walnuts and the large acorns of the mountain oak were collected each fall.

The creeks and rivers were filled with all sorts of fish. Fierce snapping turtles could be caught in caves under the riverbanks and mussels were dug from sandbars in the larger rivers.

Of course, the Cherokees had to make their living from the mountain woods. Each Cherokee, young and old, had a job to do in his village.

The men were the hunters. They followed bear and deer and mountain lion along forest trails and through tangled thickets of rhododendron and killed them with bows and arrows and stone-tipped spears. It was the men who did the heavy work of felling trees and making dugout canoes with fire and axes of stone. They cut the small trees from which the women made houses or split for basket-making. Those men who were skilled in stone-working made arrowheads and knives for the village, using brightly colored, shiny flint found on the mountainsides.

And men were the warriors. They defended the hidden villages from war parties of the Iroquois, who followed the great Appalachian Trail south-ward from the northern mountains. At other times Cherokee war parties were gone for weeks when they attacked the far-off towns of the fierce Chickasaws along the Mississippi River, and cap-tured slaves from Shawnee villages on the Ohio River, or stole wives from the towns of Creek or Tuscarora to the south and east. Every Cherokee boy was anxious to reach the age when he, too, could join a war party. Thus he would demonstrate his bravery to the young girls of his nation. Thus he would prove his manhood in the great adventure of life. The war chief of every Cherokee village was always a man.

In each Cherokee village there was also a peace chief, and this was always a woman. Her advice was listened to by men and women, boys and girls. She led the women's activity.

Indeed, all women were treated with great respect by the Cherokees. It was the mother who headed each family, and all children were members of the mother's family. When a father died or was killed in war or by a hunting accident, it was the mother's brother, or her mother's brother, who then hunted for the children and saw that they were fed and protected.

It was always this way with the Cherokees. When the white men finally came to live in the Cherokee towns and married Cherokee women, the children always considered themselves Cherokees even when they sometimes had no more than one-eighth Cherokee blood. The mother determined who and what they were.

Just as the men were kept busy each day with

manly jobs, so each girl and woman had her tasks to do. Many of the women's jobs were as hard as those of the men.

For instance, the women prepared all the food and made all the clothes for their families. This required far more work than just cooking or sewing.

All game animals brought home by the hunters had to be skinned and cleaned and cut into small pieces for cooking. This the women did with flint knives, taking care to waste nothing, as every part of an animal could be used in some way.

The hides, of course, were used to make dresses and shirts, leggings and moccasins. It was the women's job to tan the hides, making buckskin which could be sewn into soft, comfortable, warm clothing.

Basket-making was a specialty of the Cherokee women in the old days just as it is now. Even the young girls were taught to weave colorful baskets from oak splints, and honeysuckle vine and cane, dyed with the juices of berries and roots and walnut hulls.

The women made their own cooking pots from clay dug from the creek bank and grew the vegetables that went into the pots.

Mothers and daughters worked together to dig up the rich soil in the creek bottoms with bone hoes and digging sticks. Corn was planted in small hills and beans planted with the corn so that the long bean vines could climb the cornstalks as the two plants grew together. Squash was a Cherokee food, and gourds were grown to eat and to make into dishes and dance rattles.

Often the women were the doctors of the villages, although old men also cured the sick with special dances and songs and medicine made from herbs.

But all was not work among the Cherokees. Frequently villages would gather together to watch their teams play a rough game of Cherokee ball against each other. Then there were social occasions such as the many dances held throughout the year.

Each spring both men and women participated in the Green Corn Dance to ask God to make the corn grow thick and tall and fruitful. The men held hunting dances in the fall to bring them good luck in finding game. Exciting war dances were held before war parties went out against enemy villages, and victory dances were danced on the return of a successful war party.

Cherokee children most enjoyed the Booger Dance, when men would exchange clothing and put on grotesque masks carved from buckeye wood. Then they danced around the fire at night, acting like clowns, until the children guessed the identity of the men behind the masks.

When the harsh mountain winter came, and hunters could not go out in the deep snowdrifts of the creek valleys, or a chilling rain fell on the dead cornstalks in the village gardens, then the Cherokees would gather in their snug houses, around the cooking fires, and listen to the story-tellers. They would hear old men tell of how the world was made, or how the Milky Way was formed, or why the seasons changed. Old women would tell of adventures with bears when they had been berry-picking long ago, and young men would relate their exploits on some war party.

The Cherokee children listened to these stories with interest, for this was their school and their entertainment.

The fire in the middle of the floor would cast flickering shadows on the mud wall of the house. A piece of good venison might be sizzling over the fire or a pot of succotash might be gently bubbling as it cooked. The howling of the winter wind outside was like a lullaby. The voice of the story-teller speaking in rhythmic Cherokee was like music. These sounds, combined with the popping of the fire, often made the younger children drowsy.

They would fall asleep feeling that life was good, and would be good until the end of time, as long as they lived in the mountain country they loved.

And so it was, until the white man came from Europe.

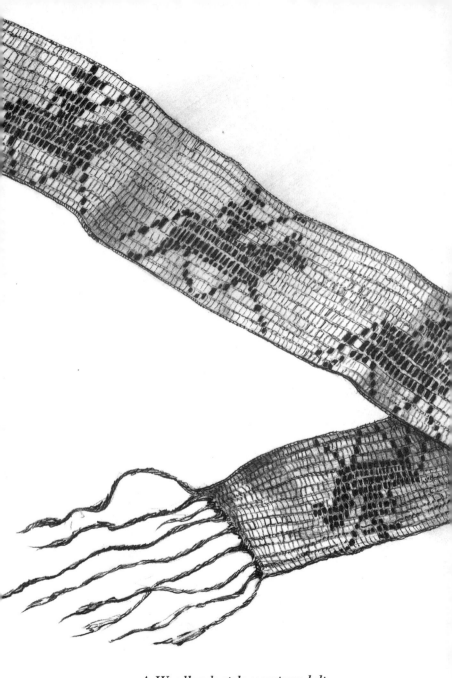

A Woodlands-style wampum belt

Spanish, French and English

▼▲▼▲▼▲▼▲

Hernando de Soto, a Spaniard, was the first European that the Cherokees ever saw. After he came, the life of the Cherokees was never again the same.

In the year 1540 de Soto led a group of Spanish soldiers up from Florida to seek gold in the North Georgia mountains. Gold was in those mountains, but de Soto and his men never found it. It was not discovered until three hundred years later, and its discovery was one of the reasons the Cherokees were finally forced to leave their beloved country.

But the Spaniards had weapons and tools of iron and steel, the first ever seen by Cherokees. Spanish knives cut easily and never broke as stone knives did. Spanish axes of iron and steel cut down a great tree in an hour, while it took the Cherokees several days to cut a tree with fire and stone axes.

Cherokee men noticed these marvelous things with great interest. They wanted the iron tools and weapons that made life so easy for the strange men with light skins.

Beneath their armor the Spanish soldiers wore soft garments of brightly colored cloth. Some wore jeweled rings on their fingers and jeweled pins on their cloaks. The soldiers had fine steel needles which made sewing much easier than the bone awls the Cherokee women had always used. Cherokee women noticed the cloth and jewels and shiny needles and wanted them.

The Spaniards were arrogant and cruel, but over the years the Cherokees liked to see the soldiers come to the mountains. Only from the white man could they obtain the wonderful tools and cloth which they could not make for themselves, but which made their lives more pleasant.

A hundred years after de Soto, Frenchmen from Canada appeared in the Cherokee country. They floated in boats and canoes down the great Mississippi, then rowed and paddled up the Ohio and Tennessee rivers until they reached the Cherokee towns in the mountain valleys.

The French were more friendly than the Spaniards. The Spaniards wanted gold and cruelly forced the Cherokees to dig for them. Frenchmen wanted furs. They brought boatloads of steel axes, needles, colored cloth, steel knives, glass beads, copper pots, mirrors and other luxuries the Cherokees had learned to want. The French traded this wealth for the skins of wolf and fox and beaver. The French brought guns, for they wanted Cherokee hunters to have good weapons so that they could hunt more easily and bring in more furs. Also the French wanted the Cherokee warriors to help them fight their ancient enemies, the English, who now had settlements in America.

English traders and soldiers from Virginia and

South Carolina followed the French, crossing the wild mountains to set up trading posts in the Cherokee country. The English also wanted furs from the Cherokees, and when they could they persuaded Cherokee warriors to fight on their side against the French.

Between the years 1700 and 1760 the Cherokees fought first with the French and then with the English. Finally they remained loyal to the English and helped them drive the French soldiers and traders from the southern mountain country.

A Cherokee clay pot, alongside an iron kettle

The Cherokees and the White Man

▼▲▼▲▼▲▼▲

By 1740, because of the white traders and soldiers in Cherokee country, the Cherokee way of life had changed greatly. Every man had a steel knife and most had iron and steel axes and tomahawks. No man even remembered how to make the old-fashioned tools and weapons of flint.

Very few women used the ancient bone awl for sewing in 1740. Steel needles, bought from the traders, were much easier to use. Almost every Cherokee woman had steel needles in several sizes.

The women still made pots from clay dug along the creek banks, and they continued to make the beautiful baskets for which the Cherokees were famous. Most families, however, had at least one copper kettle or iron pot, which would not break.

Cherokee houses had changed. The old round-houses, made of upright sticks plastered with mud, had disappeared. Now, in 1740, the Cherokees lived in log cabins built like those of the settlers. These cabins had chimneys instead of the old-fashioned smoke hole in the middle of the roof, so that one could cook over a convenient fireplace and sleep warmly on winter nights without smoke filling the house.

Instead of making clothes from deerskin the Cherokee women often traded tanned deerskins for woven blankets and colored cloth. Always, however, they continued to make moccasins from elkskin and groundhog hides. They were still a hunting people, and soft moccasins were needed to stalk animals in the woods.

Hunting was easier, too. Some Cherokee

hunters still hunted with bow and arrow or blow-gun, but many acquired guns and became dependent on the traders for gunpowder and lead bullets. Some trappers still used snares and log deadfalls to trap fur-bearing animals, but most used the steel traps made by white blacksmiths.

Many traders at this time married Cherokee women and had children by them. By the time of the American Revolution, in 1776, there were a number of prominent Cherokees with British names such as Brown and Ross, Lowrey and MacIntosh, Smith and Vann. All of these mixed-bloods considered themselves Cherokees, however, because they had Cherokee mothers. Many of them were given very good educations. Some inherited great wealth from their fathers and lived like the aristocrats of Virginia and South Carolina and Georgia.

All during the eighteenth century the Cherokees continued to make war against their ancient enemies, the Creeks to the south, the Chickasaws to the west, the Tuscaroras to the east and the Shawnees and Iroquois to the north. Sometimes they fought English settlers who illegally crossed the mountains to obtain free land in the rich Cherokee hunting grounds. Sometimes the English settlers attacked a Cherokee village and killed its men and captured its women and children.

Most of the time, however, the English and the Cherokees lived in peace. No Cherokee wanted to go back to the old, almost forgotten days when his people had no steel tools or guns or woven cloth. The English did not wish to lose the rich source of furs they found in the remote Cherokee towns. Also they wanted the help of Cherokee warriors against the Spanish, who still had settlements in Florida. The two nations lived together in a peace that none thought would end. Then came the American Revolution. That changed everything.

The Americans formed an independent nation. The Cherokees had no place in this nation. The new Americans wanted Cherokee lands, but not the Cherokees.

A Cherokee-style peace pipe

New Nation, New People

▼▲▼▲▼▲▼▲

W hen the American Revolution started, the
Cherokees sided with the English.

After all, it had been the English king who had
always protected Cherokee hunting grounds from
greedy settlers, while the settlers, who now called
themselves Americans, looked on all Indians as
enemies. The Cherokees had no reason to support the founding of the new American nation.

Cherokee warriors eagerly responded to the
English requests and took the warpath against
American settlers from Virginia to Georgia. Small
towns and lonely cabins were attacked. Men were

killed and women and children captured and taken back to the Cherokee towns, far away from their families. The Cherokees were considered devils by all the Southern frontier.

In retaliation the Americans sent fighting men to burn the Cherokee villages. Cherokee women and children were captured and sold into slavery in the West Indies, and Cherokee warriors killed. When this happened the Cherokees considered the Americans devils.

Finally the war between English and Americans was ended in the year 1783. English soldiers were sent home and the Americans ruled the land. But the war continued between the Cherokees and the new Americans, for now there was no king to keep the Americans from crossing the mountains to settle lands long coveted by them.

The Americans were rough, tough men of the frontier. They were crack shots with their long rifles and could live in the woods as well as the Indians, sleeping on the ground and killing their own food.

After the English left, bands of vengeful American fighting men drove Cherokee families from their homes and gardens, forcing them to find whatever food they could in the woods. This was not too bad in the summer, but in the wintertime when Cherokee villages were burned, families often were driven into the snowy mountains with no shelter, no food and not enough clothes.

After ten years of this cruel war the weary, discouraged Cherokees met in a great council. The chiefs, men and women, decided that they must make peace with the white man. He was too strong for them to fight, especially when the proud Cherokees no longer had the powerful armies of England to help protect them from the men across the mountains.

George Washington was now president of the new United States of America. He sent representatives to meet with the Cherokees and a treaty was signed. Since the Cherokees had lost the war they were forced to give to the Americans their vast hunting grounds in Kentucky and in large areas of North Carolina, South Carolina and Tennessee.

The Cherokees hated to sign this treaty but many of their ancient hunting grounds had already been taken over. However, the tribe still owned huge areas of Tennessee, Georgia and Alabama, the heartland of their nation. The treaty said that Cherokees could live on this remaining land "as long as the rivers flowed and the grass grew." This was not to be true, but the Cherokees believed it when the treaty was signed.

Another important decision was made at this time. The Cherokees realized that the old days of Indian freedom had gone and would never come back. They saw that the white man could not be defeated because he knew many things the Indians had never learned. The Cherokees decided to follow the white man's path, share his vast knowledge, and live in peace.

The Cherokee chiefs asked for missionaries. They did not want to become Christians but they wanted the schools that the missionaries would set up. They wished to learn how to farm and raise cattle. The women wanted to learn to weave cloth. They asked for blacksmiths to teach them to make their own tools from iron. In the years to come a few Cherokees, such as Sequoyah and Siloli, became fine workers in iron.

President Washington and the new government of the United States saw that the Cherokees were given all the help they had requested.

By the year 1800 the Cherokees were a peaceful nation. From learning the white man's ways they were becoming prosperous once again. Because many educated traders lived with them and had married Cherokee women, they felt that Cherokees and whites would now live together in peace until the end of time.

Most of all, the Cherokees hoped to avoid being moved from their homeland, a fate already suffered by many of the eastern tribes.

Woodlands-style moccasins

The White Man's Path

▼▲▼▲▼▲▼▲

A few of the Cherokees had become quite rich by 1800. One of these rich men was James Vann, whose father had been a white trader. Vann lived in a fine house in North Georgia, a house of bricks. It was built by special workmen he brought over from Europe. He owned much land on which he raised cotton and cattle, corn and hogs. He lived like rich white men, with many servants and fine furniture and books.

In 1800 Vann gave a large plot of land to missionaries from the Moravian Church. This land was called Spring Place. There the first Christian mission among the Cherokees was built. Some missionaries traveled the long distance from Connecticut to Georgia and built houses for themselves and a school for the Cherokees. Others came to the mountain country from the old town of Salem in North Carolina. They taught young Cherokees to read and write in English. Also they taught Cherokee boys to farm as the white man farmed, and Cherokee girls to spin thread and weave cloth.

The Cherokees learned the white man's ways quickly. In a few years most of them lived as comfortably as the American pioneers who had settled around them. Yet at the same time they kept many of the old Indian ways, for they were determined to remain Cherokees until the end of time.

They still hunted when they could, for they loved to hunt, but game was becoming harder to find. This meant that skins were harder to find, and cloth was needed for shirts and dresses. It meant that raising cattle and hogs for food was necessary. Farming was not so exciting as hunting, but it was easier. Indeed, it was necessary if they wished to continue to live in their ancient homeland in peace with the Americans.

In 1803, however, just when the Cherokees were recovering from the years of war with the Americans, something happened which threatened the whole future of the tribe. Most Cherokees did not understand what was happening, or that it would mean the end of Cherokee life in Georgia and Alabama before forty years had passed.

At the end of the Revolutionary War the state of Georgia was the largest of the new United States, its boundaries stretching from the Atlantic Ocean to the Mississippi River. At that time it included all the land now found in the states of Georgia, Alabama and Mississippi, most of it wilderness. About the only people living there were Creek, Choctaw and Chickasaw Indians and a few white trappers and hunters.

In 1803 the state of Georgia agreed to give up most of this land to the United States government. In return the United States agreed to remove all the Indians living there to lands across the Mississippi River as soon as this could be done peaceably. When the Indians were removed, these rich lands could be opened to white settlement.

Just a few years before, a man named Eli

Whitney had invented the cotton gin, a machine for taking the seeds out of cotton bolls. Picking seeds from cotton by hand was a very expensive process. The cotton gin, though, did the job inexpensively. It made cotton very valuable for fibers to spin into thread and weave into cloth.

As a consequence, many white people wanted these Indian lands. They wanted to cut down the age-old forests and plant cotton on the cleared land. The textile mills of England and New England bought all the cotton they could get from Southern planters and made millions of yards of cotton cloth which was sold to people all over the world at a low price. The desire for new cotton land was the first major threat to the Cherokee way of life.

In spite of this threat, the Cherokees took another big step down the white man's path in 1808. They followed a suggestion given them earlier by President Thomas Jefferson and created a strong new central government, similar to that of the United States.

The old tribal system of having many village chiefs, each responsible only for the government of his village, was discarded and one chief was chosen to preside over all the tribe. Laws were made by a council of older men, each of whom was chosen to represent a village. After this the tribe called itself the Cherokee Nation. The new government gave the Cherokees confidence in adapting to the ways of the new American nation. Many Cherokees felt that it would make them strong enough to avoid removal to the West.

Three years later, in 1811, the Cherokees proved once again that they were determined to be friends with the United States government. They were visited by Tecumseh, a Shawnee chief from Indiana who was a great orator and warrior. Like the Cherokees twenty years before, the Shawnees and neighboring tribes were feeling the pressures of the white man. Unlike the Cherokees, Tecumseh did not want to follow the white man's path. He wanted to continue to live the old Indian life of war and hunting and independence.

But Tecumseh knew that the Shawnees could not fight the white man alone and win. He dreamed of uniting all the Indian tribes of the

East against the white man. So, Tecumseh traveled all the way from the Ohio River valley to Florida, where he persuaded part of the Creek Nation to join him. Then he visited the Cherokees in their mountain capital town of Ustanali and told them how all the Indians would be left alone if only they could unite and drive back the settlers.

The Cherokee chiefs listened politely to the Shawnee orator. Then they politely refused to join him. By bitter experience they knew the strength of the white man. An army of all the Indian tribes would be powerful indeed, but the Americans were as numerous as the trees of the forest. Besides the Indians could not make the guns and tomahawks and knives needed to fight a war. They had no cannons to guard their villages, and no factories to make gunpowder.

When the powerful Creek Nation joined Tecumseh, General Andrew Jackson was sent to Alabama to fight them. About eight hundred Cherokee warriors joined the American army to help subdue the fierce Creeks, and they fought well. The Creeks were defeated, and the Cherokees returned to their mountains and continued to learn the white man's ways. Most of them thought that by helping General Jackson they had shown their loyalty to the United States. Now, they thought, the white man would leave them alone.

Unfortunately, when General Jackson was elected president a few years later, he forgot what the Cherokees had done to help him win the Creek War and he became their most powerful enemy.

But after the Creek War something strange and wonderful happened to the Cherokees. All sorts of new ideas were suddenly developed. More missionaries were invited to settle in the Cherokee Nation and more and more Cherokee children went to the mission schools where they learned to read and write and to take care of themselves and their people in the new world of the white man.

In 1817 the Cherokees became the first American Indian tribe, and one of the first nations in the world, to adopt a written constitution. This remarkable document was written in English because the Cherokees had no alphabet of their own at the time. The fact that it was written for all to see and examine, provided the Cherokee government with a stability not enjoyed by neighboring Indian nations, such as the Creeks, Choctaws and Chickasaws. It allowed the Cherokees to work together as a real nation, a united nation, in facing the threats of the future.

The new constitution called for an elected chief, like a president or governor. It called for a national court and for a small police force to keep order in each district and to arrest lawbreakers. In addition, it provided two legislative houses, like the United States Senate and House of Representatives. The elected members of these houses made the laws of the nation.

In spite of all the efforts and progress of the Cherokees, however, land-hungry whites still wanted the Cherokees removed. Once more the governments of the United States and Georgia forced the Indians to sign a new treaty giving up still more land. Some Cherokees became discouraged at this time and moved their families to the West, where the United States government gave them new land, but most of them were determined to stay in Georgia, among the mountains and valleys of their forefathers.

Shortly after the new government was established the Cherokee Nation founded a new national capital in North Georgia on the banks of the Oostenaula River. This town was called New Echota, after the old sacred town of Chota, in Tennessee, which long ago had been the capital of the tribe. Like the old Chota, it was to become the center of Cherokee culture as well as of government.

But the most remarkable thing that happened during these exciting years was the invention of the Cherokee alphabet. Because of this, almost all the Cherokees learned to read and write in their own language. This would never have happened had it not been for one man, a crippled mixed-blood born in Tennessee before the American Revolution.

This man's name was Sequoyah. He was a true genius. His story, and what he did for his people, is worth knowing.

A portion of the Cherokee Phoenix *newsp[aper]*

ᏣᎳᎩ

CHEROKEE

ROKEE

W EGHOTA, WEDNESDAY JULY 9, 1828.

PROTECTION

ᏓᎶᏂᎨ

PHŒNIX.

Sequoyah and the Talking Leaves

▼▲▼▲▼▲▼▲

Nobody knows much about the early life of Sequoyah. He was born in Tennessee about eleven years before the American Revolution. His father was a white man. Sequoyah considered himself a Cherokee, however, because his mother was a Cherokee princess, daughter of the chief of her village. It was said that the father was named Gist, or Guess, or Guest. Nobody knows who he really was, but Sequoyah was sometimes known as George Guess.

Some say that he had become lame because of a childhood sickness. Others say that his leg was crippled in a hunting accident. Regardless of the cause of his lameness, it may have been a blessing for him and his people.

Young Sequoyah could not go hunting or join the war parties of other Cherokee youths. As a consequence he learned to become a silversmith and a blacksmith. He had a shop in the Cherokee village of Tallassee outside of Fort Loudon in Tennessee. Most of Sequoyah's business must have been with Cherokees. He never learned to speak or read any English, yet he was interested in the white man and the white man's ways. He admired the many helpful tools and weapons of the soldiers and traders who lived at Fort Loudon. He was most amazed by the ability of any white man to talk with another miles away merely by sending a piece of paper with marks on it. The Cherokees called these pieces of paper "talking leaves," and many thought they were magic. Sequoyah did not. He wanted the Cherokees to have their own talking leaves.

It was not until the year 1809 that Sequoyah began to work seriously on a system of writing for his people. At that time the Cherokees had lost their lands in Tennessee and Sequoyah had moved his family to northern Alabama. In 1821, twelve years after he had started his work, Sequoyah finally developed an alphabet which could be used.

This alphabet had eighty-two characters which represented all the syllables found in the Cherokee language. Most of the letters were designed by Sequoyah. Toward the end of his work, though, he could think of no new designs. So, even though he could not speak or read English, he copied a few English letters and numbers from an English spelling book to use in his Cherokee alphabet.

When Sequoyah had finished his alphabet he showed it to George Lowrey, a rich Cherokee leader who lived near Sequoyah's home in Alabama. Lowrey was greatly excited. He took Sequoyah with him to a national council meeting in New Echota where the two of them demonstrated the alphabet.

The council realized the importance of the alphabet to the Cherokees. But before adopting it officially, they wisely asked for proof that it could be learned and would be used by most Cherokees.

To provide this proof Sequoyah and George Lowrey invited eight young chiefs from the Alabama Cherokees to come to New Echota. These young men were from the villages which still thought that talking leaves were magic and that Sequoyah was a witch. They came anyway and met with Sequoyah for three days. At the end of three days each of them had learned to read and write in his own language.

The Cherokee national council immediately made Sequoyah's alphabet official and sent Sequoyah around the nation to teach all Cherokees to read and write. Within about six months most had learned the alphabet. Thus the Cherokees became the first Indian tribe to have its own written language.

In a few months Sequoyah finished his teaching in Georgia and Alabama and traveled to Arkansas to teach the alphabet to Cherokees who had moved there. Soon the Western Cherokees and the Eastern Cherokees were sending letters back and forth across the distance which separated them.

More advantages were to come from Sequoyah's talking leaves. The missionaries soon had textbooks, Bibles and hymnbooks printed in Cherokee. In 1827 the Cherokee government adopted another constitution written in Cherokee instead of English. Now all Cherokees could read Cherokee laws.

Later, in 1828, a national newspaper was started. It was named the *Cherokee Phoenix,* after the bird of Greek legend that sprang to life after it had been consumed in fire. One of its purposes was to unite the Cherokee people. Another was to develop support from whites in order to help the Cherokees fight removal.

The *Phoenix* was printed in English and Cherokee. It was circulated among all the Cherokees and to many, many white people all over the world. It had a number of subscribers in England, that country with which the Cherokees had been allied for so many years before the American Revolution.

In just thirty years, then, the Cherokees had progressed from a group of hunters and warriors to a "civilized" nation. They could read and write in their own language and thereby learn the white man's ways much more quickly than other Indian nations, which had no written language. They had a republican form of government and had laws written in their own language. They had schools and books and a national newspaper. Much of this remarkable progress was due to the crippled blacksmith Sequoyah, and his talking leaves.

A detail from a carved stone pipe

Hope and Despair

▼▲▼▲▼▲▼▲

I n 1828, the great John Ross was elected princi-
pal chief of the Cherokees. Under his leader-
ship the Cherokee Nation reached the high point
of its history, and later suffered its greatest
tragedy.

Ross was an elegant, blue-eyed mixed-blood,
the son of a white trader and a Cherokee mother.
He was a well-educated man, and devoted to the
welfare of his people.

By the year 1828, there were many fine homes
and farms owned by Cherokees and mixed-
bloods. In addition to the outstanding Vann

house at Spring Place there was the comfortable house of John Ross near Chattanooga, the
huge house of Major Ridge, another Cherokee
chief, and other houses as fine as any owned by
rich white men. Barns had been built for live-
stock, and neat fences of split rails surrounded
many Cherokee fields. Impressive herds of cattle
and hogs were owned by Cherokee farmers who
had once been hunters. No longer did the people
depend on the dwindling supply of wild game for
their food.

Several good roads, one called the National
Road, had been built within the Cherokee Nation
by this time. Thus it was easy to bring goods into
the nation and ship cotton and other farm goods
out to markets in Georgia and Tennessee. Steam-
boats, owned by Cherokees, operated on the
Coosa and Tennessee rivers. Cherokees could sell
farm goods to the world in return for money,
which is needed for any nation to grow and become strong and independent.

New Echota, the national capital, had grown
into a thriving town during the nine years since its

founding. It had several government buildings, a courthouse, a council house, a printing office, a number of stores and three taverns. Some of the missionaries and a number of Cherokees had built fine houses there.

With all their progress, though, the Cherokees were fiercely proud of the old traditions which kept them Cherokees.

Comfortable moccasins were still worn instead of the stiff, awkward shoes of the white man. The hunter was still respected as in the past. The old dances still took place in the spring and fall, and Cherokee ball was still the favorite sport.

By this time, too, the Cherokees thought that finally they had learned the secret to a comfortable, civilized life — to live and let live. But the secret was no good unless everyone, white and Cherokee alike, felt the same way. Unfortunately this was not true.

In the same year that Ross was elected chief, Andrew Jackson was elected president of the United States. Also in 1828, near the Cherokee mountain village of Dahlonega, a Cherokee boy found a small nugget of gold, the treasure old Hernando de Soto had sought three hundred years earlier. Many Cherokees did not realize it at the time, but the combination of President Jackson and the discovery of gold eventually made it impossible for the Cherokees to stay in their beloved mountains.

A Cherokee-style carved wooden "booger" mask (Used in ceremonies, these masks were sometimes made as caricatures of the Cherokees' enemies.)

President Jackson and the Gold Rush

▼▲▼▲▼▲▼▲

A ndrew Jackson had been a great general before he was elected president. He had defeated the powerful British at New Orleans in the
War of 1812. Later, with the help of the Cherokees,
he had defeated the fierce Creeks at the Battle of
Horseshoe Bend in Alabama. His armies had always
been made up of frontiersmen who had fought Indians since before the American Revolution. Many
of them had seen members of their families killed
and captured by Indians. Because of this they hated
all Indians. Besides, they had always coveted the
fertile Indian lands across the mountains.

Andrew Jackson was the hero of these rough, tough, brave frontiersmen. He too had been born in a log cabin and reared on the frontier, where his family had fought Indians. Jackson did not like Indians any more than the land-hungry frontiersmen did.

When the first gold nugget was found in the mountains near Dahlonega the Cherokees thought very little about it. They were happy and prosperous, with no need for gold. Cherokees had never understood why the white man, starting with de Soto, had always wanted gold.

But all through history men have fought and killed and stolen for gold. It represents wealth and wealth brings power. White men outside the Cherokee Nation were very much interested in hearing that gold had been discovered there. They started the first gold rush in the United States.

Many of the gold miners were rough, cruel men. They paid no attention to laws or treaties or the rights of Cherokees. Cherokee families were driven from their homes and gold hunters took over the neat cabins. The miners stole the food from Cherokee gardens and killed Cherokee cattle and hogs. Cherokee men who tried to protect their families were beaten or even killed by the miners.

Appalled by what was happening, Chief Ross immediately sent in Cherokee marshals to drive the gold hunters from Cherokee lands. There were too few marshals, however, and too many white men. More and more miners invaded the Cherokee Nation.

Ross then appealed to President Jackson. He asked the president for United States army troops to close the gold camps and to stop white men from killing Cherokees and stealing their cabins and food. Under the last treaty signed by the Cherokees the president was supposed to protect the Indians and their lands, with soldiers if necessary. Jackson sent so few troops, however, that he might as well have sent none. The handful of soldiers could do no more to control the robbery and murder than the Cherokee marshals.

The governor of Georgia, knowing that Jackson

would not stop him, used this opportunity to send militia troops into Cherokee lands. But, the Georgia troops protected the miners instead of the Cherokees and actually helped the miners drive Cherokees out of the gold fields. Then the state of Georgia began to pass a number of laws aimed at forcing the Indians out of the state.

One law made it illegal for a Cherokee to mine gold, even on his own land. Another stated that Cherokees could not testify against white men in a court of law. The worst of the white men could burn and steal and murder all they wanted and would escape punishment in the Georgia courts. But if a Cherokee killed a white man while defending his family, he would surely be hanged for murder, and the Cherokee government was powerless to interfere.

Even more humiliation was heaped upon the Cherokees when the Georgia legislature passed a law claiming that the whole Cherokee Nation was only another county in Georgia and subject only to Georgia laws. This selfish act completely ignored the constitution and laws of the Cherokee

Nation and all of the treaties between the Cherokees and the United States government. Georgia state officials were sent into every part of the Cherokee Nation to take over its government, and Georgia militia troops protected these officials with muskets and cannons.

Outraged by these acts, John Ross hired a famous lawyer in Philadelphia to take the Cherokee case before the United States Supreme Court. The court ruled that the new Georgia laws were illegal, and the Chief Justice, John Marshall, immediately ordered President Jackson to send United States troops to Georgia to move all white men from Cherokee lands.

Andrew Jackson, however, refused to obey the court's order. "John Marshall made the ruling," Jackson said. "Let him enforce it." This statement encouraged even more white men to move into the Cherokee Nation.

When all this happened, old Chief Junaluska, the Cherokee leader who had helped Jackson fight the Creeks at the Battle of Horseshoe Bend, said, "If I had known this would happen I would

have killed Jackson that day at Horseshoe Bend."
But Jackson was very much alive and determined
to use his high office to help drive the Cherokees
from the state of Georgia so that white men could
take over Cherokee lands.

Not all of the people of Georgia agreed with
what their state government was doing to the
Cherokees. Many people from all over the country objected strongly to President Jackson's atti-
tude, but the political forces behind Jackson were
more powerful than the friends of the Cherokees.

In the next few years the Georgia legislature
passed more laws against the Cherokees. Among
the worst of these was the Cherokee Land Lottery
Law of 1832, by which the state sold all the Indian
lands in North Georgia to white men. According
to this new Georgia law, no Cherokee was allowed
to own land in the state.

Some white families moved in immediately to
take over the farms they had won in the lottery,
driving off Cherokee families who had lived on
the land for generations. Other whites took over
farms which had been abandoned by discouraged

Cherokees who had moved on to Arkansas. Some of the new owners waited patiently to claim their farms when all the Cherokees were moved west.

During this period there was much fighting between Cherokees and white men, with many deaths and much suffering on both sides. The peace the Cherokees had hoped to have by following the white man's path was lost. The fine Cherokee government with its written constitution and schools was unable to operate effectively. Soon, only six years after it had been founded, even the *Cherokee Phoenix* could no longer be printed.

The poor Cherokees, so proud of their remarkable progress, were frustrated and angry. Chief John Ross and members of the national council traveled frequently to Washington, pleading with president and Congress for help in keeping the beautiful mountain country which had always belonged to the Cherokees.

But then the Cherokees became divided among themselves, and what happened made all of the efforts of John Ross and other leaders useless.

In the year 1835, at a time when Ross was in

Washington, a group of only three hundred Cherokees, led by rich Major Ridge and the former editor of the *Phoenix,* Elias Boudinot, met and signed a new treaty with the United States. This infamous treaty stated that the Cherokee Nation had agreed to give up all its lands in Georgia and Alabama, and to move all its people to new lands in the wild country west of the Mississippi River.

A treaty signed by only three hundred Cherokees was quite illegal according to Cherokee law and treaties with the United States. Only a majority of the seventeen thousand Cherokees could legally make such an important decision. Yet this treaty was accepted eagerly by President Jackson. In 1836, the United States Senate decided by one vote to approve it. Once the Senate had voted, all hope for the Cherokees was lost.

Some whites wanted to allow Cherokee families to own one hundred sixty acres each in Georgia. Many would have stayed in Georgia if they could have kept their farms. Andrew Jackson, however, personally took this provision out of the treaty.

So, no more would Cherokees fish for trout in

the cold mountain creeks. Never again would the drums and rattles and songs of the Green Corn Dance echo from the mountainsides. The brilliant colors of autumn leaves, which covered the mountains like a Paisley shawl, would no more be seen by Cherokee eyes.

Chief John Ross was dismayed by this treaty and continued to fight it, but he could do nothing but delay the actual removal for three more years. At this time some Cherokees voluntarily moved their families to the West, but most could not believe what had happened. They continued to farm and hunt as they had always done until the year 1837, the last year of the Cherokee Nation in Georgia.

Andrew Jackson was no longer president in 1837. President Van Buren, however, carried out Jackson's policy of removal. In the fall of the year, when the bears were fattening for the winter and Cherokee corn was being harvested, Van Buren sent United States army troops to the Cherokee Nation. He ordered them to collect all the Cherokees living there and move them under guard to Arkansas.

A Cherokee-style woven shoulder bag

The Soldiers Come

▼▲▼▲▼▲▼▲

Now came the time of sorrow for the Cherokees. Now came removal to the West, where the evil spirits of Cherokee legend dwelt.

Soldiers came into the nation from every direction. Some marched over from Augusta and some came down the National Road from Nashville. Each soldier carried his musket and bayonet and pouch of bullets. With the soldiers came great wagons loaded with tools and food and ammunition. Officers in bright uniforms, swords at their sides, rode prancing horses at the head of their marching troops. The heavy wheels of cannons rumbled along the rough roads which wound through the valleys and across the mountain passes of Cherokee land.

At night the soldiers camped along the roads, their fires gleaming in the thick woods. Far from home, they sat around the fires and listened to the owls and wolves and raccoons and panthers which prowled through the forests on the mountainsides.

When the soldiers arrived at their destinations they built great stockades of huge split trees set upright in the ground. Around the inside walls they built rough huts in which the Cherokee families could live, for the cold mountain winter was coming on. Here, in these prison camps, the Cherokees would be kept while they waited to be marched to the West.

Then, when the stockades were built, and firewood had been cut for the winter, and army rations stored at each of the stockades, the soldiers were sent out to gather in the Cherokees.

This was not an easy job. Some of the Cherokees lived near roads, but most lived deep in the mountains in small coves where no road could be built. The only way to reach most of the Indian cabins was by a narrow woodland trail. Often there was not even a trail and the soldiers had to wade up mountain creeks to reach some of the Cherokee homes.

The Cherokees were given no chance to do more than gather a few clothes and cooking pots and baskets of corn before they were marched to the stockades. Some were eating when the soldiers came, and they were not even allowed to finish their meals.

Sick persons were forced to get out of bed and dress and march to the stockades with the rest. Old people were prodded with bayonets if they did not move quickly enough. Sometimes Cherokee men tried to protect their families and were knocked down and beaten by the soldiers.

Some of the soldiers took what they liked from the Cherokee cabins. Others killed chickens and hogs and cattle for their own food.

Often families which had won land in the Cherokee Lottery came with the soldiers. The last view of home many Cherokees had was of white people moving into the neat houses and barns that the Cherokees had worked so hard to build. The fields they had cleared with so much labor and the fences they had built from split chestnut logs were left forever.

Some soldiers tried to help the Cherokees as much as they could. One wrote about his experiences years later. He said, "I fought through the Civil War and have seen men shot to pieces and slaughtered by the thousands. But the Cherokee Removal was the cruelest work I ever knew."

A few of the Cherokees managed to escape the soldiers by taking their families on hidden trails which led from the Georgia mountains to the wilderness of the Great Smoky Mountains. There the soldiers could not find them.

There was one Cherokee named Tsali Wasituna, or Charlie Washington, who could not bear to see the soldiers hurt his family. While marching to a stockade a soldier mistreated Tsali's wife. Tsali killed this soldier and he and his family quickly ran into the woods and managed to escape to the Great Smokies. Later Tsali was to become one of the heroes of the removal.

Most of the Cherokees, however, were imprisoned in the stockades.

Soon the winter came. It was particularly cold in that winter of 1837–1838. Many of the Cherokees had very little food, and Cherokee women did not know how to prepare the flour given them by the army. They were not allowed to go out of the stockades and hunt, for the soldiers were afraid that the hunters might escape. Often the firewood gave out and Cherokee children and old people shivered in the crude huts inside the stockades. Many died from disease and exposure and malnutrition.

When spring finally came, the weakened, weary Cherokees were told to prepare for the long march to Arkansas. Before leaving, the soldiers tried one more time to capture the few families who had escaped to the Great Smoky Mountains. They were unsuccessful. Finally they agreed that if Tsali and his family would give themselves up, the other families in the mountains could remain.

Tsali and his sons were brave men. One morning they surrendered to the soldiers and were executed by a firing squad of Cherokee men who were forced to do this dreadful task. Only the youngest son, a small boy, was saved. Then the soldiers marched, leaving about a thousand Cherokees to start life again in the Great Smokies.

These few were the only Cherokees who stayed in their beloved mountains. They once more built cabins and cleared small gardens in the hidden valleys of the high mountain ranges surrounding the Oconee Luftee River and its tributaries. Their descendants live there still, close to the graves of the brave Tsali and his sons.

When the spring of 1838 arrived, and the mountainsides were painted with a mist of fresh green and geese were flying north, the Cherokees were told to prepare for the long journey to Arkansas. About five thousand started by boat down the Tennessee River to the Mississippi, and then up the Arkansas River to their place of exile. It was a cruel journey, supervised by soldiers who cared little about the health and welfare of their captives.

The heat of summer came early that year and

the hot summer sun brought much sickness. The boats were crowded and uncomfortable. To make things worse, some of the government contractors, who were to supply food to the Cherokees, were dishonest. They supplied rotten meat and weevily corn, much of which could not be eaten. So hunger was added to the discomfort and sickness which afflicted the poor Cherokees.

Chief John Ross heard of the suffering of this first group of Cherokees to leave Georgia. Ross got permission from the army to delay the departure of the rest of his people until cool weather. He hoped to prevent more sickness and death by this delay.

Most of the remaining Cherokees left Georgia in October 1838. This last party went overland, instead of by water. Wagons carried the few belongings of the Cherokees as well as sick people, old people and young children. Some of the more prosperous Cherokees rode horses, but most of them walked the thousand miles or more to Arkansas. The route they took went through Tennessee and Kentucky, across the southern tip of Illinois, then through Missouri to the western part of Arkansas.

Unfortunately, that winter was exceptionally bitter. The freezing winds were worse for the Cherokees in Ross's party than the summer heat had been on the first party to leave. Food was scarce, as earlier travelers had killed most of the game along the route. There was no shelter along the way; no help from anyone.

The Cherokees sometimes walked through driving snow for days on end. Many of the rivers and creeks they crossed were frozen, and there were no bridges. When the parties halted at night they slept on the icy ground with only thin blankets to protect them.

As a consequence, many old people and children grew sick and died along the way, and were buried in shallow graves dug in the frozen earth. The rich died along with the poor, and even Chief John Ross lost his beloved wife, and was forced to bury her in a strange land and face his bitter exile without her. One out of every four failed to survive the long, hard journey.

The graves of the dead were like teardrops falling on a sandy trail, lost and forgotten as the

Cherokees moved on. This cruel journey is still known among the Cherokees as the "Trail of Tears."

In Arkansas the Cherokees tried to start over again. They built new cabins, cleared new fields, cut and split logs to make new fences. The unfamiliar country was not the same as home, however. The Osage Indians, who had always lived in Arkansas, resented the new invaders and fought them. The Cherokee government never became as strong as it had been in Georgia. There was no established national capital like New Echota, no newspaper, no hope. There was only courage.

In Georgia, after the Trail of Tears, most traces of the remarkable Cherokee Nation disappeared. The Cherokee mission schools were torn down, and the town of New Echota was destroyed. The land where the council house and the taverns and the missionary houses had once stood was made into fields. All traces of the proud capital were plowed under like the rotting stalks of last year's corn.

Now, in all of Georgia and Alabama, there is nothing left of the nation that had lived there for a thousand years before the white man came. The Cherokees are gone, pulled up by the roots and cast to the westward wind.

They are gone like the buffalo and the elk which once roamed the mountain valleys. They have disappeared like the passenger pigeons which once darkened the sky as great flocks flew over the river routes from north to south and back again. Like wayah, the wolf, and like the chestnut trees, the Cherokees are no longer found in the mountains of Georgia.

Now only the names remain: Dahlonega, Chattahoochee, Oostenaula, Etowah, Nantahala, Tennessee, Ellijay, Tallulah, Chattooga, Nacoochee, Hiawassee, Chickamauga, Tugaloo, Chattanooga . . .

I N D E X